Waiting
in Gratitude

COLLECTED PRAYERS
OF WALTER BRUEGGEMANN

Acting in the Wake: Prayers for Justice

Following into Risky Obedience: Prayers along the Journey

Waiting in Gratitude: Prayers of Joy

Waiting

in Gratitude

Prayers of Joy

COLLECTED PRAYERS OF
WALTER BRUEGGEMANN, VOLUME 3

WALTER BRUEGGEMANN

WITH BARBARA DICK

WJK WESTMINSTER
JOHN KNOX PRESS
LOUISVILLE • KENTUCKY

© 2024 Walter Brueggemann
Foreword © 2024 Westminster John Knox Press

First edition
Published by Westminster John Knox Press
Louisville, Kentucky

24 25 26 27 28 29 30 31 32 33—10 9 8 7 6 5 4 3 2 1

Scripture quotations from the New Revised Standard Version of the Bible are copyright © 1989 by the Division of Christian Education of the National Council of the Churches of Christ in the U.S.A., and are used by permission. All other biblical quotations are the author's paraphrase or translation.

Excerpts from "O Lord My God, How Great Thou Art," words by Stuart K. Hine, © 1949, 1953 The Stuart Hine Trust CIO. All rights in the USA its territories and possessions, except print rights, administered by Capitol CMG Publishing. USA, North and Central American print rights and all Canadian and South American rights administered by Hope Publishing Company. All other North and Central American rights administered by The Stuart Hine Trust CIO. Rest of the world rights administered by Integrity Music Europe. All rights reserved. Used by permission.

Book design by Drew Stevens
Cover design by Mary Ann Smith

Library of Congress Cataloging-in-Publication Data is on file
at the Library of Congress, Washington, DC.

ISBN-13: 978-0-664-26828-2

CONTENTS

Foreword by Deborah Krause   ix

Preface to Volume 3   xv

ONE: PRAYERS OF JOY IN *LIFE*

For the Family   2

Emilia's Confirmation   3

For Shannon and Jonathan
(On the Occasion of Their Wedding)   4

Corinne and Jim . . . from Their
Mothers' Arms (Wedding Day!)   6

Love Lived Forward (For Nina and Marius)   8

For Jeff Crittenden   11

For Tad and His Tribe of Healers
(Dr. James "Tad" Wilson Jr.)   13

Remembrance of Bob Hanson   14

Invocation   17

At Installation (For the Installation
of Elizabeth Rechter as Rector)   19

At Installation (On the Installation
of David Stabenfeldt and David Schnepf)   21

Called . . . and Kept in Goodness   24

Charge to Stacy Midge (Jeremiah 20:7–13)   27

Risking Our Secrets   30

Mike's Last Saturday at Timberridge   31

Thanksgiving for Charlie . . . after Fifty Years!   34

On Considering Gunkel   37

Our Interpretive Task   38

Many Singing Saints   40

Weeping until Dawn (On Reading Psalm 30)   42

Waiting in Gratitude   44

Prayers of the People   46

For the Sake of the World   48

The Nominating Speech
(On Reading Psalm 146)   50

Prayer of Thanksgiving at the Table   53

On Our Way Rejoicing   56

TWO: PRAYERS OF JOY IN *CHRIST*

Earth's Scarred Yearning (Luke 24:36–43)   60

On Reading Exodus 7–12   62

Poor Pluto   64

On Reading 1 Samuel 5   67

One More Day in Our Birth Process	68
On Reading Isaiah 4:2–6	69
Jesus Loves Me, and Us, and All the Little Children	70
Joy amid Hurt	72
Before We Eat	73
Invocation at the Eucharist	74
On Reading Jeremiah 31:31–34 (DMin Day 8)	75
All Things Hold Together	77
On Reading Isaiah 6	78
For Your Reliabilities in Our Lives	79
From Parsimony to Abundance (Genesis 12–50)	80
On Generosity (A Chapel Prayer)	82
Loaves Abound!	85
Easter Tuesday	87
Full of Grace and Truth	88
Marveling at Your Sovereign Goodness	90
Overwhelmed by Promise	92
On Reading Psalms 96; 107	93
Awed in Gratitude	95
TGIF!	96
Soon!	98
On Reading Samuel	100
On Priestly Legislation	101
Beginning with Jeremiah	102
Unlike Us!	104

Gathered in Astonishment
(On Reading Acts 10:44–48)   106

Scripture Index   109

FOREWORD

⌘

The saying attributed to Augustine, Luther, and John Wesley that "to sing is to pray twice" has another application among theological educators — that is, to pray before class is to lecture ten times. As privileged students of Walter Brueggemann and his colleagues at places like Eden Theological Seminary and Columbia Theological Seminary, we would hang on the prayers of our teachers. Their practice of prayer before lectures and seminars and for special and ordinary occasions would inflame and inform our imaginations to be bold before the throne of grace. Among none has this been more true than for Professor Brueggemann.

For most of us the exercise was a powerful performance that would astound and convict, and for a few it played its intended role of vocational formation. A dear colleague and onetime student of Professor Brueggemann, the Rev. Dr. Martha Robertson, now emerita professor of contextual education at Eden Theological Seminary, continues, with renowned skill, to hone the craft of prayer learned from her seminary professors. Once I asked her how she did it. How are her prayers so vivid, honest, present, gorgeous, and arresting? "I practice paying attention," she said.

"I keep notes on experiences, language, and events. And I relish the chance to delight God and others with what I share in prayer."

Delighting God is the "chief end of humankind," according to the Shorter Catechism of the Westminster Confession of Faith, which begins, "What is the chief end of humankind? To worship and enjoy God forever." In their practice of prayer, Martha and our professors show that this posture of paying attention to God in life can result in having the power of prayer. In other words, that possession is not so much a gift as it is a fruit born of practice, nurtured by everyday devotion.

Think of Serena Williams practicing the toss of her serve hundreds of times a week, or Wayne Gretzky skating and handling the puck for hours on end. That level of devotion, when practiced by the gifted, yields greatness. The foundation of it all is much hard work, sometimes tedious effort. In the legacy of Walter Brueggemann's teaching, writing, and praying, of which this trilogy of volumes is an archive, we see the fruit of this discipline of devotion. He makes it look easy, or at least like second nature, but do not miss that it is a harvest of a lifetime of hard work grounded in paying close attention to life and God in purposeful communities of learning and faith.

Professor Brueggemann's preface to this volume makes clear that this collection's focus on joy is not a denial of pain and suffering in our lives. In fact, the Psalms, which provide so much of the textual basis for his prayers, often link lament, woe, and complaint with thanksgiving and joy shared with God. Why does he have to emphasize this link? Because too often the rhetoric of contemporary popular Christian piety proclaims a facile victory over lament that is not scriptural and indeed is idolatrous. Turn to the Prophets, Psalms, the Gospels, and the letters of Paul, and see that lament and praise, suffering and deliverance, agony and ecstasy are bound together in a dialogue of faith. To repress the expression of this struggle is to eclipse the space of grace honed by God's people as we give voice to our fear, pain, and grief in the midst of our hope in God.

This volume shares prayers in two sections: joy in life and joy in Christ. The two categories (much like lament and praise) overlap, and yet the distinction is instructive. Professor Brueggemann notes that his particular vocation has provided varied opportunities to pray publicly in the events of the everyday life of a father, grandfather, theological educator, friend, and person of the church. The prayers gathered here that, much like Scripture, dive into the specificity of marriages, baptisms, retirements, ordinations, and installations showcase the presence of God encountered up close, in people's lived lives, in Walter's lived life. The intimacy of these glimpses of family, friends, students, and colleagues held before God and God's redeeming love are bread crumbs to the work of paying close attention and discerning God's presence and purpose in all our lives and living, whatever is happening and wherever we are. We are invited not merely to observe in general, but also to follow along in all the details of our contexts and lives.

The category of joy in Christ offers testimony to the practice of faith that is trust in God's redeeming love at work in the ministry of Jesus and his death and resurrection. The apostle Paul used the Psalms and Prophets to illumine how the practice of this faith yields space for joy (Phil. 3:1, 4:4). Brueggemann's prayers arise from his exegesis of biblical texts, like Jeremiah 31:31–34 and Isaiah 4:2–6, engaged in the context of his teaching on particular occasions. This is his ministry, his priestly bearing of oil in the midst of his congregations of students, readers, and listeners. Each prayer offers evidence of how the painstaking devotion of careful attention to sacred texts, lives, and situations yields insight into God's inbreaking saving grace and the eruption of joy it brings— always specific to the time and full of the hope that resists fear in its myriad toxic and looming expressions of cynicism, cruelty, grievance, and death. Indeed, "there is a balm in Gilead!"[1] And if you don't know what "Gilead" means, look it up. There will be a measure of grace for you in the effort, Brueggemann teaches us.

To learn from Professor Brueggemann, be it in the classroom, the keynote lecture, the commentary, the article, or any one of his many books, is to witness regularly and yet somehow also astonishingly the activation of the Bible's witness of a myriad of ways to wrestle a blessing from God. These prayers, and those of the other two volumes, are particular performances of that activation. Yes, as performances, they entertain, amaze, and even delight, and they are aimed in this current collection ultimately to teach. Pray as Walter Brueggemann does, not because you can, but because if you try, you will know joy.

Deborah Krause
Eden Theological Seminary

Notes

1. African American spiritual, "There Is a Balm in Gilead," *Glory to God* (Louisville, KY: Westminster John Knox Press, 2013), #792. Future references to *Glory to God* are abbreviated *GtG*.

T his collection of my prayers is marked by *joy*: gladness of faith concerning the reality of God, the wonder of God's work, and the abundance of God's good creation. For those readers who know my previous work, it will be recognized that I have focused very much of my energy and attention on the laments (complaints) of Israel—prayers of urgent need. Such a reader may wonder if, with this accent on joy, I have turned away from my long-running focus on laments. But my current focus on joy is not at all turning away from laments. And the reason is this.

As Claus Westermann (*Praise and Lament in the Psalms*) already has shown, with a few notable exceptions, Israel's *laments* dramatically move toward and end in *joy, thanks, and an assurance of being heard*. Thus, the recurring dramatic structure of Israel's laments is that the one who laments becomes certain that, in response to an urgent petition, God has heard and will answer. That responsive intervention by God (which is regularly implied in the Psalms) allows and causes a dramatic reversal from lament to joy. We may cite three exemplars of this transformation that evokes joy.

1. In Psalm 30 the psalmist affirms:

Weeping may linger for the night,
    but joy comes in the morning.

v. 5

The move is from weeping to joy. And then the psalmist narrates the dramatic exchange that leads to the transformation:

- a petition is voiced that asks God to hear (vv. 8–10);
- it is affirmed that God has acted decisively to "clothe me with joy" (v. 11);
- the transformation evokes loud praise and thanks (v. 12).

2. It is evident that Israel's exodus narrative is patterned in the same way. The narrative begins in desperate lament:

After a long time the king of Egypt died. The Israelites groaned under their slavery, and cried out. (Exod. 2:23)

The following narrative reports on YHWH's repeated emancipatory actions. The narrative concludes with the exuberant joy of Miriam and the other women:

Sing to the LORD, for he has triumphed gloriously; horse and rider he has thrown into the sea.

15:21

Thus the movement from weeping to joy is the same as in Psalm 30.

3. In the Fourth Gospel, the reassuring words of Jesus move in the same way:

> Very truly, I tell you, you will weep and mourn, but the world will rejoice; you will have pain, but your pain will turn into joy. When a woman is in labor, she has pain, because her hour has come. But when her child is born, she no longer remembers the anguish because of the joy of having brought a human being into the world. So you have pain now; but I will see you again, and your hearts will rejoice, and no one will take your joy from you. (John 16:20–22)

Again there is an abrupt reversal from *pain* to *joy*.

In all three instances, the conclusion is one of joy (Ps. 30:5; Exod. 15:21; John 16:20–22). But in all three usages, the affirmation of joy is preceded by a full acknowledgment of weeping, groaning, and pain. In each case, the negative reality is transformed by the faithful power of God who makes possible the great inexplicable gift of joy. Prayers of joy appear at the end of the dramatic processes when the community of faith (and its members) are rescued and emancipated by God from troubles with which they could not themselves cope.

As is evident in this collection of my prayers, however, not all of our prayers of joy arise from lament resolved. Many of these prayers arise from our marking, treasuring, and appreciating specific moments of significance that characterize our shared lives. Because I am elementally a churchman, many of these prayers are markers of special occasions in the life of the church. This includes a prayer for Jeff, for David (along with William), for Stacy, and for Mike in their ministries, and for dear Charlie on his fiftieth anniversary, for installations that mark beginnings in ministry of Elizabeth, the two Davids, and my well-beloved colleague Bill Brown.

The circle of the church happily overlaps with the circles of our families and zones of our lives. The God to whom we pray is the one

> who, from our mothers' arms,
> hath blessed us on our way
> with countless gifts of love,
> and still is ours today.[1]

As a result, included here are prayers for the confirmation of my dearly beloved granddaughter Emilia; for the weddings of Shannon and Jonathan, Corinne and Jim, and Nina and Marius; the medical ministry of Tad; the continuing study of John; a remembrance of Bob Hanson at his death. As we name particular persons, we are mindful of how greatly we treasure them:

> For the joy of human love,
> brother, sister, parent, child,
> friends on earth, and friends above,
> for all gentle thoughts and mild:
> Lord of all, to thee we raise
> this our hymn of grateful praise.[2]

And just to be inclusive, there is a grateful mention of Hermann Gunkel (1862–1932), the godfather of my kind of scholarship from the University of Halle, who died the year before I was born but whose work and influence linger mightily.

Beyond that, there is in these prayers a wide, deep practice of gratitude for the mundane matters of our life that are received as gifts from God: bread, family, book, persons of courage, singing saints, and the wonder of ministry. These prayers savor the particularities of our lives. In an early story, John Updike has his protagonist ponder the Eucharist. The lead character in the story concludes, "The world is the host; it must be chewed."[3] These prayers are a glad "chewing of the world" as we mark and celebrate its concrete freighted reality. The sum of these prayers is to voice our life back to God in wonder and gratitude for God's "countless gifts" that are indeed beyond our counting. We nevertheless continue to count them! We name them one by one. And with each naming we are dazzled by the abundant generosity of this generous, self-giving God. It is for this reason that our prayers inescapably spill over with lyrical rhetoric that defies explanation or quantification. Our words are, at their best, scarcely adequate for what we receive, know, and trust in gratitude.

Finally, we arrive at complete joy. The church, beyond ministry and family, ponders the unutterable reality of Christ, the embodied reality of the self-giving God of the gospel. "Joy in Christ" is the watchword of Paul in his letter to the Philippians. Indeed, Paul can hardly find adequate words for his confident delight in the presence and power of Christ. So he writes to the church:

> Finally, my brothers and sisters, rejoice in the Lord. . . .
>
> Rejoice in the Lord always; again I will say, Rejoice. (Phil. 3:1; 4:4).

This joy is "finally," after everything else has been said and done. "Finally" there is the wonder of Easter and the gift of new life. This joy is "always," in every circumstance. That "joy always" for Paul is marked by prayer, supplication, and thanksgiving (4:6), and culminates in "the peace of God" (v. 7). Before he finishes his letter, Paul brings his joy down to the actual practice of the congregation:

> I rejoice in the Lord greatly that now at last you have revived your concern for me; indeed, you were concerned for me, but had no opportunity to show it. (v. 10)

Paul is mindful of the specific persons to whom he writes and finds delight in their faithful generosity toward him. Indeed, their generosity is for him a "fragrant offering, . . . acceptable and pleasing to God" (v. 18). In his deep joy, the distinction between *mundane human acts* and *confidence in God* is readily blurred. It is all one, because joy is no time to sort things out. Deep joy, rather, is to take the sum of all that we are and have and have received as a gift with gratitude that is as boundless as God's own goodness.

It becomes clear that the practice of prayer, specifically prayers of joy, can be no *add-on* to an otherwise lived life. Such joy can be no ingredient in a life of fear, greed, hate, or violence. That is because such joyous prayer is not an *elective* that we may choose for the edge of our existence. It is, rather, a new *center for all of our life from which arises all of the practices commensurate with God's own goodness:*

> The fruit of the Spirit is love, joy, peace, patience, kindness, generosity, faithfulness, gentleness, and self-control. (Gal. 5:22–23)

As I complete this triad of collections of my prayers, I am grateful to the community of those who have been my long-running partners in prayer. Among them are generations of seminary students and many pastors who day by day, "when other helpers fail and comforts flee,"[4] speak prayers of hope, comfort, and reassurance. Such good pastoral work marks in our common life both births and deaths, and many freighted moments in between. The work is to continue to uphold the world with prayer, a quaint but determined insistence that the world does not consist in *wealth*, *wisdom*, and *power*, but in the practice of *love*, *justice*, and *righteousness* (Jer. 9:23–24).

Walter Brueggemann
Columbia Theological Seminary

Notes

1. Martin Rinkart, "Now Thank We All Our God," trans. Catherine Winkworth, *GtG*, #643, st. 1.
2. Folliott Sandford Pierpoint, "For the Beauty of the Earth," *GtG*, #14, st. 4.
3. John Updike, "The Music School," in *The Early Stories, 1953–1975* (New York: Random House, 2012), 418.
4. Henry Francis Lyle, "Abide with Me," *GtG*, #836, st. 1.

ONE

PRAYERS OF JOY IN *LIFE*

God of all our years,
   we are this night filled with gratitude
   for all the ways in which you have kept us and
      blessed us.
   We give you thanks for all the years that stretch
      from ancient Bertha
      to the youngest among us tonight.

   We give you thanks for our dead whom we
      remember as we treasure them.
   We give you thanks for all those in our family
      who are marked by integrity,
      bravery, and faithfulness.

   As we part company tonight,
      we pray for your mercy upon us,
      that you will keep us safe and well until we
         meet again.

And before you finish, we pray that you will bring
your work
      of justice,
      of freedom, and
      of peace
   to your whole creation.
We pray in confidence of your mercy. Amen.

   —July 28, 2007, Hallman Family Reunion, Kansas City

Lord Jesus,
    We pray your blessing on your beloved disciple,
       Emilia,
          that she may be not only smart, but wise;
          that she may be not only strong,
             but compassionate;
          that she may grow into maturity,
             to love you as you love her . . .

fully,
without reservation,
forever. Amen.

—June 4, 2017

(On the Occasion of Their Wedding)

You birth us and we reach out for nourishment;
We grow alone and crave companionship;
We sleep and wake,
  hunger and eat,
  work and rest,
  and yearn for embrace.

And then, wondrously, you break that cycle of solitude:
      You open your heart to love us,
        You love us from all eternity . . . and beyond
          that . . .
You make love real and concrete and daily and intimate
    by giving us to each other,
    by letting us give love and receive love
      and be bound in love that defies all our
          loneliness and
    the long creep of our death.

On this day we give thanks
for Shannon and for Jonathan,
      for their families who loved them to this day, and
        for their courage and passion and hope.
        We pray rich joy for this twosome,
          and beyond this twosome to their neighbors.
        We pray them glad obedience to your call,
          that what is intimate and what is public,
          that what is gift and what is task,

may flourish in your mercy and goodness
all their days.

Bless them, and through them bless your world
in justice and peace,
in mercy and forgiveness,
all in the name of your love enfleshed in Jesus.
Amen.

—July 25, 2005

(Wedding Day!)

Now thank we all our God
with heart and hands and voices,
who wondrous things hath done,
in whom this world rejoices;
who, from our mothers' arms,
hath blessed us on our way
with countless gifts of love,
and still is ours today.

We give you thanks for Corinne and Jim and your
countless gifts of love to them,
whom you have blessed from their mothers' arms;
you have watched over them, brought them to full
life and healthy adulthood,
     and now to mutual love for each other;
you have provided them with food, shelter,
and safety until now,
     and we ourselves have abundant food here for
          which we thank you.
You have given them families who love them
and call them by name;
you have given them good work to do,
and wisdom to do it;
you have crowned their lives with goodness,
and we thank you.

O may this bounteous God
through all our life be near us,
with ever joyful hearts
and blessed peace to cheer us;
and keep us in God's grace,
and guide us when perplexed,
and free us from all ills
in this world and the next.

You are a bounteous God;
we pray that you will be near Corinne and Jim
each day,
keep them in your grace, guide them when perplexed,
and free them from all ills of body, mind, and spirit.
For all this and for Corinne and Jim in their new life
we give you all praise.

All praise and thanks to God,
who reigns in highest heaven,
To Father and to Son
and Spirit now be given:
the one eternal God,
whom heaven and earth adore,
the God who was, and is,
and shall be evermore.

With thanks and praise and joy and well-being,
we pray. Amen.

*—November 26, 2016. Hymn text from Martin Rinkart,
"Now Thank We All Our God," trans. Catherine
Winkworth, GtG, #643.*

(For Nina and Marius)

For the beauty of the earth,
for the glory of the skies,
for the love which from our birth
over and around us lies:
Lord of all, to thee we raise
this our hymn of grateful praise.

For the joy of human love,
brother, sister, parent, child,
friends on earth, and friends above,
for all gentle thoughts and mild:
Lord of all, to thee we raise
this our hymn of grateful praise.

For thyself, best gift divine
to the world so freely given;
for that great, great love of thine,
peace on earth and joy in heaven:
Lord of all, to thee we raise
this our hymn of grateful praise.

God who loved the world into being,
    Who sustains the world by your faithful love,
    Who is the impulse of all of our human love,
We thank you for the deep layers of love
that have brought us to this day:

For families and for generations
who have loved each other through thick and thin,
For parents, grandparents, sisters, and brothers
who surround Nina and Marius,
And for their new love for each other.
We thank you for Nina and the grace-filled woman
she has become,
And for Marius and the grace-filled man
he has become,
And for your providential care
that has brought them to this moment of vows
of fidelity and a new relationship.
We come to ask your good blessing on their
new life together.
That they may find abiding joy and well-being
with each other,
That they may remain, each of them, a strong
generative person,
And that together they may build a fresh presence
for well-being in the world.
Grant that their new life may blossom into a force
for good,
That they may give their lives over
beyond themselves
To the good work of love and justice
and reconciliation in the world.
Bless each of the families with the joy of a new son
And the joy of a new daughter.
Let these two blessed people so live
that the world around them may see
the goodness and mercy of God.

We commend them to you for safekeeping,
    That their lives may be faithful witnesses
    to your loving living presence in the world.

We pray in the name of Jesus who is perfect love
among us.
Amen.

*—June 18, 2016, Columbia Theological Seminary. Hymn
text from Folliott Sandford Pierpoint, "For the Beauty of
the Earth," GtG, #14.*

God of all generosity,
   who blessed the plants and animals in creation,
   who blessed Abraham and Sarah on their trek
      into newness,
   who blessed Jacob amid his wrestling,
   who blessed kings and prophets and priests,
   who blesses the church in its ministry,
Now bless Jeff and cause your face to shine upon him
   in gladness, and courage, and wisdom.
Receive our common thanks for Jeff, his life,
and his ministry,
   for his liberated imagination,
   for his courageous leadership,
   for his love of learning,
   for his passion for your word and your work, and
   for his practical wisdom about faithful life
      in the world.
You who withhold nothing needed from your people,
   Grant to Jeff an overflow of your Spirit,
      that he may relish his life,
      that he may soar in his work,
      that he may enter honestly into all the dark places,
         and celebrate your gifts that well up there,
      that he may be a blessing as he is blessed.

And give him peace . . . peace that passes all human understanding,
  in the name of Jesus who passes all our
    understanding,
      in his life, his death, and his life beyond all
      deaths. Amen.

—December 3, 2015

(Dr. James "Tad" Wilson Jr.)

You are the Great Healer;
You transform, restore, make new . . .
   and summon and demand.
      You leave us with residues of pain,
      and scar tissues of hope.
You recruit human healers in your healing crusade.
   We give you thanks for doctors
      with healing hands who probe and diagnose,
      with healing ears who listen for our "deep breath,"
      with healing eyes who watch our reflexes snap
        . . . or not,
      with healing words that speak truth in love.
Among them we give thanks for Tad,
   for the discipline of his craft,
   for the artistry of his caring,
   for the generosity of his practice,
   for the ways in which he makes a difference.
You, with Tad and all of his tribe of healers,
   remind us of the gift of life in its abundance,
   and of the possibility for well-being even amid
     our flawed frailties.
When we ponder you, and Tad and his ilk,
we are glad that
   "The Doctor is in!"

—December 30, 2013, Columbia Theological Seminary

Our lives are given to us as free gifts.

> We treasure our lives,
> > sometimes in gratitude,
> > sometimes in self-preoccupation,
> > sometimes in compulsion and regret.

However we live, we eventually come to its end.
> We are plunged into death,
> > and we are pressed beyond
> > > our control,
> > > our resources, and
> > > our power or our skill.

Beyond all of our explanations, we are pressed beyond ourselves
> into the depth of death.

When we arrive in that mystery, we find it marked
> by love,
> by acceptance,
> by mercy, and
> by generosity.

In death we plunge our lives into the mystery
of love, acceptance, mercy, and generosity.

> And now we mark Bob's life as it is plunged in the
> same way

into that mystery of love, acceptance, mercy,
and generosity.

Our lives are free gifts that we treasure,
and Bob's life has been a free gift that he treasured,
and that we now treasure.

We treasure Bob as we remember him:
for his love of out-of-doors;
for his steadfast care of the earth;
for his resolve and his investment in good earth policy.

We treasure Bob for his curiosity and his eagerness
to know the latest in scientific knowledge;
for his compulsive sense of fairness and his
indignation at unfairness;
for his unfailing devotion to his family that he
loved best and most;
for his long years of service toward those with
special needs.

We treasure Bob for his gifts and skills and compe-
tences as a healer;
as a devoted husband, father, and grandfather;
for his unwavering sense of who he was,
and how he wanted to live his life.

And now we consign him, at the end of his life,
to his entry into death,
there to be enveloped for all time and beyond time
in the abiding mystery of love, acceptance,
mercy, and generosity.

We voice our thanks for his life,
and we acknowledge our loss and sadness in his death.
    We resolve in this moment of fondness and
        gratitude
    to live from his legacy
        that we will love all of our neighbors
            as he also loved.

We pray all of this into the mystery of love where he
now dwells forever.
Amen.

—August 24, 2013

INVOCATION

God of all kinds of mothers and fathers in this place,
  we come, after them, in thanksgiving.
  We give you thanks for all those who have
    taught and studied and worked here,
      the timid,
      the diligent,
      the courageous,
      the anxious,
      the daring.
We are their daughters and sons,
      and carry in our midst all of their habits.

We give you thanks for the present company of
  teachers and students and staff . . .
  good comrades and troublesome friends.
Especially do we give you thanks for Bill,
  a child of your promise,
               and for Gail,
  a carrier of your goodness and
  guardian of her treasured daughters.

From him we have taken you to be
  God of the eons and of this moment,
  God of scrolls and of crickets,
  God of spiders and saints,
    of all things great and small.

This night we gather among your faithful witnesses,
    alongside your many creatures,
        receiving life from you,
        inhaling hope,
        handling texts,
        on the alert for your presence.

Good God of mercy and truth and justice,
    as we gather,
        gather with us,
        gather us your people into your goodness,
    that our praise may turn to obedience,
    that our joy may turn to mercy,
    that our Easter may turn to Pentecost power,
    that we finish faithful, glad,
        with hearts toward you,
    the one we know through Jesus
        whom we confess. Amen.

> —*October 23, 2007, on the inauguration of*
> *William P. Brown to the Columbia faculty*

(For the Installation of
Elizabeth Rechter as Rector)

Folks have been coming to St. Mary's forever,
    it is the same old, same old,
    same ways of doing things,
    same places to sit,
    same songs to sing,
    same factions and parties and groups,
    same Lord Jesus, all unchanged,
        forever and ever.

Elizabeth, our priest, comes new among us,
    but with conviction and passion
        and habit and pattern.
And now newness for all parties,
    newness for St. Mary's,
        to be led where it has never been before,
    newness for Elizabeth,
        beyond what she knew or thought or even felt.

Newness from God who makes all things new;
Newness from the Spirit who blows where it will;
Newness from the living Lord who bids us follow;
Newness required by an old world ending
        and a new one not yet traceable.

Fresh waves of violence,
    unprecedented quotas of fear and anxiety,
    unanticipated and inexplicable fractures
                in the public fabric . . .

And this priest is to stand up and speak news
      about love and mercy and compassion and justice;
And this congregation is to act newness
    toward immigrants,
    and prisoners,
    and all the forgotten,
    even the monied, powerful forgotten
      who yearn for something else.

All this we offer, good God of newness,
All this we ponder while we pray.
    Begin us again beyond ourselves;
    Revive us again beyond our habits;
    Breach what is old and tired and in dispute.
Surprise us all,
    Raise us up,
      that we may be an Easter force
        in a world gone deathly.
    Raise us up, and we will finish,
        bold, singing, dancing,
          embracing, hoping . . .
    toward you and beyond ourselves,
    from you and toward neighbor.
    Raise us up as you have indeed raised Jesus to
    new life.
    Amen.
                —*March 26, 2006, St. Mary's Episcopal Church,*
                              Maryville, Tennessee

(On the Installation of
David Stabenfeldt and David Schnepf)

You have called us into the church,
   to accept the cost and joy of discipleship.
You have called from among us
     pastors and teachers,
     priests and prophets,
     women and men,
     entrusted with the tradition,
         and the vision,
         and the imagination to lead your
            church into newness.

On this day, we give thanks for your call among us
     to David and
     to David,
that they should be among us to enact
Word and sacrament,
         memory and hope,
   that we may be more fully and faithfully your people.

We give you thanks for them,
   we give thanks for this church,
     for its long stream of faithful people,
     for mothers and fathers in faith,
     for long years of mercy and compassion
        and generosity and caring.

With them—and in the company of that great cloud
of witnesses—
    we give you thanks for our call to mission,
        to be your faithful witnesses,
        to be led by your Spirit,
        to resist the powers of evil,
           and to share in Christ's baptism and death.

We expect and pledge to be led by your leadership
        and we expect to follow . . .
    Except . . . we have our moments of recalcitrance
      and stubbornness;
    Except . . . we have our streaks of resistance and
      do not want
                to follow easily;
    Except . . . we are variously frightened and inclined
          to be hard-hearted,
            tilted toward selfishness and slander
            and parsimony and prejudice.

So here we are . . . on this wondrous occasion . . .
    glad for these new pastors,
    joyous to be your church,
    but aware of how it is among us.

All we can do then in this hour
    is to hope for your Spirit of newness among us;
all we can do today
    is to pray to be our better selves;
all we can do
    is to center our lives on your wisdom
        and pray to be made new, all of us together.

All we can do
     is to seek forgiveness for how we have been,
        and walk into your newness.

You are our God and we are your people;
     we are ready for your newness that heals
        and lets us walk into mission.
We make our prayers in the name of Jesus
     who is our good Savior and Lord. Amen.

*—April 23, 2006, St. John Evangelical
United Church of Christ, Collinsville, Illinois*

CALLED . . .
AND KEPT IN GOODNESS

About you, Holy God, we have heard this said:
    "We know that all things work together for good
    for those who love God, who are
    called according to his purpose" (Rom. 8:28).
We are grateful for your **good purpose** in the world,
    that you intend the world to be a venue
        for peace, justice, mercy, and compassion.
    On this special day, we pray to situate David
        afresh
    in that good purpose,
        that his gifts and passion may be mobilized
        for your good purposes.
We are grateful that we may **love you**,
your name, your purpose, your future;
    We love you dearly and without reservation,
        loving you back for the elemental love
        with which you uphold us.
    On this special day, give good measures of your
        love to David
    even as he loves you with all his heart.
We are grateful that **we are called** to your good purpose.
    We give you thanks that all of us in the church
        have received that call,
    that our lives may be bent
    toward the good work of peace and justice in the
        world.
    On this special day, we give thanks that David is
        called.

His call has been through
   many toils and snares.
   But now, on this happy occasion,
   we affirm his call joyously and unambiguously.
We are grateful that for all of us called to your purpose
   that **all things work together for good**.
   We cherish that assurance in the midst of our
      awareness
   that things are not good . . .
      seasons of alienation and abandonment,
      of economic disappointment and depletions of
         health,
         but we affirm that all things are in your
            purview for good,
         all things of body, heart, and soul,
         all things material and spiritual,
         all things personal and public,
            all things . . . because you hold the whole
               world in your hands.
   On this special day, we pray good in all things
      for David.
      Good in his health,
      Good in his economics,
      Good in his shared life with William,
      Good in his pastoral casting,
      Good in his dark nights and in the light of his days.
We commend him to you in love and affection,
   Confident of his gifts,
   More confident of your faithfulness.

We pray all this in the name of Jesus,
    Lord of the church,
    Lord of our lives,
    Keeper of promises,
    Giver of blessings. Amen.

—April 29, 2018

⁓

(Jeremiah 20:7–13)

Beloved Stacy: For your charge I offer you the passionate prayer of Jeremiah 20:7–13, a text appointed for today's lectionary:

1. Jeremiah prays in angry honesty to God:

> O Lord, you have enticed me,
>   and I was enticed;
> you have overpowered me,
>   and you have prevailed.
> I have become a laughingstock all day long;
>   everyone mocks me.
> For whenever I speak, I must cry out,
>   I must shout, "Violence and destruction!"
> For the word of the LORD has become for me
>   a reproach and derision all day long.
> If I say, "I will not mention him,
>   or speak any more in his name,"
> then within me there is something like
>   a burning fire
>   shut up in my bones;
> I am weary with holding it in,
>   and I cannot. (vv. 7–9)

I charge you to pray deeply and honestly to God from whom no secret can be hid. Pray hope and pray despair; pray love and pray bitterness. As Jeremiah was seduced into his vocation by God, there will come times when you will know that God tricked you into coming to Mt. Auburn where you do not want to be. Pray it all!

2. Jeremiah prays to God concerning his adversaries, perhaps with a little paranoia:

> For I hear many whispering:
>   "Terror is all around!
> Denounce him! Let us denounce him!"
>   All my close friends
>   are watching for me to stumble.
> "Perhaps he can be enticed
>   and we can prevail against him,
>   and take our revenge on him."
> But the LORD is with me like a dread warrior;
>   therefore my persecutors will stumble,
>   and they will not prevail.
> They will be greatly shamed,
>   for they will not succeed. . . .
> Let me see your retribution upon them,
>   for to you I have committed my cause.
>   (vv. 10–12)

I charge you to be honest with God about your adversaries, especially the ones close at hand, the ones who expect too much, the ones who stubbornly disagree about everything, the ones who pay your salary. Name them, and then give them over to God and move on. Let your adversaries be a burden for God, not for you. Relinquish them to God.

3. Jeremiah prays in honesty and then finishes
   with a fresh doxology:

Sing to the LORD;
   praise the LORD!
For he has delivered the life of the needy
   from the hands of evildoers. (v. 13)

I charge you to let your vexations—about God who
seduces and about adversaries who trouble—to be
enveloped in and contained by doxology, praise that
is the complete and glad abandonment of self to the
wonder of God.

I charge you to live and pray in **honesty** with God,
   in ready **relinquishment** of your adversaries to
   God, and in glad **abandonment** to the wonder
   of God. And be thankful!

—June 25, 2017, Columbia Theological Seminary,
Mt. Auburn Presbyterian Church

RISKING OUR SECRETS

⦿⦿

Lord of our wounds, master of our hopes, ruler of both our rage and our joy, we turn our lives to you because we have no other way to be honest in ways that make a difference. You are the God from whom no secret is hid; so we will, as we are able, voice all of our secrets to you. We ask that you receive them gently and tenderly, break them open for new possibility, and hand them back to us as sources for new life. As we pray our secrets in confidence to you, we stand alongside many sisters and brothers who have secrets as well. We join with them in our need and in our hope. We know about tears in the night and joy in the morning; we offer our nights of tears and our mornings of joy to you in thanks and trust. Amen.

—July 13, 2017, for John Cloete
as he continues his study of the Psalms

You are the God who upholds
   the long large arc of creation,
   and who commits nanoseconds of redemption.

You are the God of large, abiding purpose,
   who pauses for the sake of the struggles
      of those who are not yet with the program.

You are the God who lives amid wondrous doxology,
   but who stops the song in order to hear
                              the cries of the needy.

You are the God who ministers for and among us,
   and calls us to the cost and joy of your ministry.

We thank you that we are named to ministry in our
            baptism as children of your promise;
We thank you that we are nurtured to ministry by
         bread broken and wine poured out;
We thank you that,
by the specialness of the laying on of hands,
         you call some to Word and sacrament . . .
      And on this day
We thank you for Michael and his call
                  to Word and sacrament,
                  Michael baptized as child of
                  promise,

Michael broken in ministry like
bread broken,
poured out in ministry like you are,
Michael empowered by hands
laid on and by Spirit.

So we mark his gifts in thanksgiving this day,
his patient listening,
his caring presence,
his passion for renewed church,
his openness to those who differ,
his delicate way of good order
and generous spirit,
his wise move from care to
program to ministry,
his truth-telling directness
and his gentleness that marks his
truth.

At this great turn in his life, our prayers are for his
well-being,
his joy,
his safe travels and
courage for what lies ahead.

He, Michael, is among your earthen vessels,
and we celebrate his culmination of ministry
in this place,
we ponder the trace of the gospel he has
preached among us . . .
the reality of love and recognition and forgiveness
and justice and mercy and peace,
given to him . . . and through him to us all.

Yours is the ministry of the coming kingdom;
we have glimpsed
    that coming kingdom in the ministry of Jesus and
        in Michael's witness to Jesus.
And we give you thanks. Amen.

> —*July 31, 2005, Timberridge Presbyterian Church,*
> *McDonough, Georgia*

You are the God who gives
    and gives and gives,
  and you have given us the treasure of the gospel.
   For this treasure by which we live,
     we give you thanks,
    for summons to obedience,
    for words of forgiveness,
    for acts of generosity,
    for miracles of newness,
    for promises that "all things will be well,"
  for your very self, given in death
             and
    raised again to life.

For this treasure we give you thanks for
    earthen vessels that offer your news,
     for book,
     for towel,
     for table,
     for cup,
And on this day, for your child Charlie,
      a clay pot . . .
        well worn,
        with chipped edges, and
        scarred decorations . . .

But Charlie, all these years
    of priesting,

with courage and candor,
with wit and irony,
with steadfast love and gentleness,
with starchy truth-telling and
   buoyant hope-telling . . .
This clay pot who has given
   goodness out of his wounds, and
   assurances out of his doubts, and
   newnesses wrenched from his own
      weariness.

We are grateful this day for Charlie . . .
   and for Betty,
      who has lived all this time
         with this irascible priest,
      knowing the foibles and hurts,
         and losses and rages,
   and who has hung in with generous,
      demanding fidelity.

Fifty years of earthen vessels!
Fifty years of faithful caring!
Fifty years of hope amid despair,
            of honesty amid flimflam,
            of humor amid dread,
Fifty years,
   enough for Jubilee.

And so we say with ready tongues and glad hearts,
>   Jubilate for the treasure!
>   Jubilate for these two earthen vessels!
>   Jubilate for good news come fleshed among us!
>   Jubilate!
>   Jubilate!
>   Jubilate!
> Come, Lord Jesus . . . amid our need,
>   our expectation,
>   our joy . . .
>   Jubilate! Amen.

—December 17, 2006, in celebration of Charlie Roper's fifty years of faithful ordination

We do love to tell the story,
    because we have the sense that it is true,
    because its cadences ring true about us and our lives,
    because in telling and hearing,
        we draw close to you in your hiddenness.
So we thank you for your readiness,
    to occupy the story,
    to move the story from problem to resolution,
    to stay faithfully in the plot of the story.
We crave and cherish and ponder the plot.
We find you always surprising,
    sometimes surprising in absence,
    sometimes surprising in power,
    sometimes surprising in mercy,
    but always you as the Key Character.
Give us the courage to trust this account of our life,
              to rest our present and
              to risk our future
    on this story that is the narrative
    of You, of Jesus and his wondrous love. Amen.

—February 12, 2001, Columbia Theological Seminary.
Hermann Gunkel (1862–1932)
was a German Old Testament scholar.

OUR INTERPRETIVE TASK

We give you thanks for the text-messages that you
    have sent us,
      even as we marvel that you have given yourself
        to us in the Book,
      and that you have remained hidden from us in
        the Book.

We give you thanks for the bold and courageous
    text-makers,
      even while we acknowledge the uncommon cruelty
        of some of the characters in the text.

We give you thanks for fanatics and fundamentalists
    who have kept the text for us,
      even while we own our identity as daughters and sons
        of ancient, vicious, interpretive wars.

We give you thanks for the parade of witnesses and
    interpreters
    whose heirs we are,
      even while we acknowledge that their work is
        deeply contextual,
      even while we are tempted to absolutize their work.

We give you thanks for our task as interpreters,
    for the gift of imagination,
    for the hard work of competence,
    for the demanding disciplines of fidelity.

Give us courage for our work,
    and enough modesty to see our work
        as provisional and penultimate.

We pray in the name of the word come flesh,
    even while we cherish the word come print.
        Amen.

*—April 14, 2008, Columbia Theological Seminary Old
Testament Theology Class*

We were glad when they said to us,
   "Let us go to the house of the Lord."
   When we got there,
   we discovered that there were many, many
     people there,
     just like us, ready
       to trust and obey.
We were pleased when they said to us,
   "Let us go there singing,"
   and when we started singing praise to God,
   we discovered that there were many people
     singing in harmony
       who are quite unlike us:
         conservatives singing with liberals,
         gays with straights,
         men and women . . . of course,
         Europeans, Asians, Africans, and lots of
           white folk just like us,
            singing in a thousand tongues,
              our dear redeemer's praise.
We exulted when they invited us to find a psalm
   for each of our brothers and sisters,
   and we discovered that the book is
   big enough in scope,
     for all of us and each of us to have a psalm

Just for me!:
> One a doctor,
> One a queen,
> One a shepherd in pastures green,
> One a soldier,
> One a priest,
>> Others in school,
>> Or in the lane,
>> Or at sea,
>> Or in a shop or on a train
>> Or at tea.

Each singing, all singing,
as long as we have breath,
as long as we live . . .
A mighty chorus of praise and self-abandonment,
all singing,
all trusting,
all obeying,
all loving God,
all loving neighbor,
all being loved beyond the end of time,
By the God given us in the good, good gospel.
Amen.

—October 10, 2012, St. Timothy Church, Cincinnati, Ohio

(On Reading Psalm 30)

You are the one from whom no secret can be hid.
Before you we give ourselves over in honesty.
 And so we weep:
 We weep at loss and hurt;
 We weep at disappointment, even to despair;
 We weep local stuff like broken promises and
  failed bodies;
 We weep public stuff,
  Too much violence,
  Too much poverty,
  Too much homelessness,
  Too much deathliness,
 Even while we benefit from it all.
We weep air through the night, when the old ghosts
return, and you seem remote. We weep in honesty
and confidence because we know you treasure our
every tear. You gather all of our weeping into your
own Friday grief.

And then . . . sometimes at dawn . . . joy comes!
 Joy comes as healed body or restored relationship;
 Joy comes in new policies that redress injustice;
 Joy comes as you give new life when we could no
  longer manage.

In your gift of joy,
   We want to dance,
   We want to praise,
   We want to thank.
And all of our dancing and praising and thanking
are taken up by you in your Easter news:
   The lost found,
   The dead raised,
   The hurt healed,
   The sin forgiven.
We are your Friday people in grief;
We are your Sunday people in joy.
We yield ourselves back to you,
   In gratitude,
      and then in obedience.
      Amen.

   —April 10, 2013, Columbia Theological Seminary,
            St. Timothy Church, Cincinnati, Ohio

We are thankful for warm homes and caring families —
    and too much to eat!
We are thankful for the breaks and the rests
    and the gifts that come from you.
We are mindful that much of what we covet
    comes to an end
    because of your sovereignty.
We are mindful of your haunting promises of
    new beginnings.
    We know that your beginnings are filled with
        surprise,
    and sometimes with dread and terror for us.
We do better to covet that which does not end
but endures,
    but our more immediate desires pull and tug at us
        as we prepare for your coming.
We thank you for your faithful church,
    which all this time has been waiting and hoping.
    It has given us a venue for your cost and your joy,
    your burden and your amazement.
We do our waiting along with your whole church,
    with less than honest repentance,
    with less than eager longing.
We give thanks that your coming is
    not extrapolated from our honest repentance,
    nor is your arrival geared to our eager longing.

Thus we are bold to pray, as our mothers and fathers
have long prayed,
   that you will come . . . willy-nilly. Amen.

—November 19, 1976

We pray to you, giver of bread,
     pourer of wine,
     giver of life,
     ruler of the world.

In your presence we gather our whole memory of
life with you,
 all its miracles and gifts and wonders.
In your presence we gather our whole hope of new
life from you,
 gifts marked by forgiveness and generosity,
  by hospitality and well-being,
  and finally by justice.

In your presence we gather, as we are able,
all of our needs;
 we name before you our deep hungers
  and hope for your wondrous food,
  hunger for companionship,
  hunger for mercy,
  hunger for peace,
  hunger for discernment and courage.

We name before you
 the homeless and the cold,
 the sick and the dying,
 the despairing and weary,
 those who live in places of violence
  and those who perpetrate violence.

Receive from us our weary, war-torn,
worried world as we hand it to you;
    bless it,
    break it,
    and give it back to us transformed.

We wait to receive such healing transformation
from you;
    we watch the bread,
    we notice the wine,
    we trust your promises;
        by the time we finish, we inhale
            your newness for us and give thanks. Amen.

—January 20, 2008, January Adventure,
St. Simons Island

We dare to address you,
    You God,
    You God before us,
    You God after us,
    You God coming and going in freedom among us.
We present ourselves to you in the company of your saints,
    that company that stretches through time and
        through space.
We give you thanks for all of your saints over time,
    and most especially those wondrous contestants
    for social justice and transformation,
        most particularly Rauschenbusch and Niebuhr
        and Cone and Ruether
            and all their company.
    We thank you for their courage in action
    and their daring in imagination.
We give you thanks for the sweep of space,
    for the prophets and apostles, saints and martyrs
    right now around the world.
We give you thanks for the saints among us
    who mostly go unnamed and unnoticed,
    but who persist for the sake of your good kingdom.
We are their daughters and sons,
    and their vision and adrenaline persist among us.

So we ask you to make present among us
   that same energy and courage for transformation
   in, with, and under us
   that we may fully resolve to make a difference
   for the well-being of our world.
As we pray for your mercy and justice and
well-being,
   So we also resolve to give ourselves over to it.
Receive now our thanks for these good days together.
Let us return to our ordinary lives with fresh resolve
   and new courage,
   that we may be useful in your purposes of
   well-being,
   and engage with the powers of death
   for the sake of your gift of life in the world.
We pray for the sake of the world that you love.
We pray in the name of your bodied love,
      Jesus of Nazareth. Amen.

—January 19, 2013, Columbia Theological Seminary;
January Adventure, St. Simons Island

(On Reading Psalm 146)

Here we are at the great convention;
>We may end up like Democrats with only one
>candidate;
>For now we are like Republicans with dozens of
>choices.

We live among many candidates for God:
>The church,
>The party,
>Our wealth,
>Our race,
>Our gender,
>Our nation,
>Our physical appearance,
>Our moral goodness.
>>Each of them with an appeal. Each of them
>>demanding our attention.
>>Each of them making promises it cannot keep.

By the end of the process . . . we have listened to
too many advocacies and been seduced by too many
options.

Only one talked differently. Only one candidate did
not pander to us.
That one talked mercy and compassion and justice
and reliability.

That one told us stories of old deliverances and recent rescues.

The name, as in every nominating speech,
was withheld until the end of the speech.

And then, like a torrent of assertions:

Yahweh,

Yah,

Yah,

Yah.

And we opted for Yah!

That God with compassionate power,
Devoted to mercy for immigrants,
Pledged to compassion for widows,
Vowed to justice for orphans.

No other candidate had focus on
widows, orphans, and immigrants,

Not our party,

Not our ideology,

Not our race,

Not our gender,

Not our nation.

And so, when we heard, "Yah, Yah, Yah,"
We readily answered, Hallelu,

Hallelu,

Hallelu.

We did not say Hallelu-democrat or -republican.

We did not say Hallelu-America or -China.

We said the only thing that made sense. We voiced:
Hallelu-Yah.

We fingered the miracles.
We named the rescues.
We celebrated the healings . . .
   the lame,
   the blind,
   lepers,
   the deaf,
   the poor.
And then we remembered where we had witnessed
all of this . . .
   In this Jesus
     who enacted Yah.
And so we voted Hallelu-Yah.
We voted for Jesus.
We signed on for his campaign.
We followed him . . . gladly.
   Gladly for we knew then and we know now,
Hallelu . . . it is Yah who makes happy. Amen.

—*June 3, 2015, St. Timothy Church, Cincinnati, Ohio*

PRAYER OF THANKSGIVING AT THE TABLE

We come to you in thanksgiving for
our remembered past
    that teems with your wondrous gifts.

    We have this large inventory of
        prophets and apostles,
        martyrs and saints
        who risked everything for your purpose.

    We have this local memory of parents and
        teachers and pastors,
        all kinds of adult guardians who have watched
        over us until now.

    We have this strange holy One —
        truly God, truly human —
        before whom we bow in adoration, even Jesus.

We come to you in thanksgiving for our anticipated
future
    for we do not doubt that he will come again
    and that the kingdoms of this world
        even the savage nations
        even our own powerful nation
    will become the realm of our God and of his Christ
        who will come with peace.

We come to you in thanksgiving for our present moment
- beset as we are with anxiety and weariness
- anxious as we are about the world
  and our place in it
and yet knowing that this time,
  like every time, is in your hand.

In this posture of thanksgiving, we give you thanks for these tokens of bread and wine, and ask for your mighty Spirit to come upon them and upon us, that this brokenness and poured-outness may sign us fully as your people. And now we pray as we have been taught:

Our Father . . .

On the night of his arrest when he was handed over for execution,
our Lord Jesus took bread . . .

The costly gifts of God for the grateful people of God.

Let us give thanks —

we have come to you in hunger . . . and are dazzled always again by your gifts of bread and wine, body and blood, your gift of self

that outruns our need. We depart this table
   full and satiated with you,
   marked by your brokenness that
      we may engage the brokenness of the world,
   marked by your poured-outness
      that we may let our lives be poured out
         in justice and mercy and compassion,
         in wonder, love, and praise. Amen.

—March 4, 2005

We give you thanks for this day and its mercies,
for good companions,
for truth spoken openly,
for visions of what might be,
and the mustering of energy for tomorrow.

While we might wish for three booths here,
we are on our way again,
carrying some fresh visions and new energy,
but also situated more honestly
in the call you voice to us.

We are on our way again,
back to our places of life and love and work,
back to hard-hearted, unthinking people,
back to those who mean well but who
do not catch on,
back to those who know better than do we,
and summon us always beyond ourselves.

We give you thanks for the whole people of God
in this place and in every place.
We give you thanks for wise bishops,
for faithful pastors,
for thoughtful teachers,

and for the whole company of the faithful . . .
  those who exhort in exhortation,
  those who give in generosity,
  those who lead in diligence,
  those who are compassionate in cheerfulness.

We know all about fear and fatigue and anxiety;
  but just now,
    what we know is thankfulness:
      We thank you for our common
      creatureliness;
      we thank you for our call to faith;
      we thank you for our good neighbors
      in justice and peace;
      we thank you for our commonwealth
      of democratic freedom
        and hopes of justice.

Most of all, we thank you
    for your grace that outflanks us,
    for your truth that sustains us,
    for the fullness of your self
      in Friday suffering and Sunday wonder.
Abide with us
  as we pledge to abide with each other . . .
      and with you. Amen.

— *September 25, 2007, Wisconsin Council of Churches,*
Stevens Point, Wisconsin

TWO

PRAYERS OF
JOY IN CHRIST

(Luke 24:36–43)

We arrive in your presence
 yet again scarred,
  by old hates,
  by failures that haunt,
  by our violations that remain unforgiven,
  by hopes disappointed,
  and hungers left unfed.

 We arrive scarred and yearn
  for your light and wholeness and presence
         unflawed.

And then you . . . you in your unexpected coming,
  your coming when we have quit hoping,
  your speaking wholeness amid our brokenness,
  your liveliness among us marked by Friday.
 You let us touch your wound,
    your scar,
    your bruise;
 We finger it and let its scabbiness
    rub against our lives.

We discern in you scars that give healing, and
    wounds that are filled
     with mercy, and
    bruises blue and marked full
     with compassion.

You overwhelm us with your suffering love,
   and we find our lives made whole by
                  your resilient presence.
You are the bodied mystery of new life
                  given via suffering.

By your address to us,
   we are empowered
      to reenter our wounds and
         notice newness there,
      to revisit our old hungers and be fed there,
      to reengage oldnesses unforgiven,
   and there to find your gift of new life.

We leave your presence made whole,
                  not unbruised,
                  not without flaw,
                  not without wistful
                     disappointment . . .
   But now yours,
      yours beloved,
         restored,
         forgiven,
         healed,
   And sent again into the world that you love.
      Amen.

—April 30, 2006

Great God, sovereign, Lord —
    We attest your splendor as creator of heaven and
      earth;
    We confess your power as emancipator of your
      slave people;
    We affirm you bodied from Nazareth, full of
      grace and truth;
    We gladly assert that you hold the whole world
      in your hands.
And then we read more closely —
    We notice your big promises are thick with tiny
      gnats;
    We observe that your big miracle is
      accomplished through slimy frogs;
    We are astonished that your purpose is airborne
      in flies.
Your great engagement on our behalf
    is not only to slave huts;
        not only to widows, orphans, illegal aliens;
        not only to publicans and sinners;
        not only to such as us in our privilege,
        But tiny, slimy, and airborne;
        But via gnats, frogs, flies.
No wonder sister Miriam sang and danced . . .

> The songs of justice,
> the dances of freedom,
> the croak of frogs,
> the sting of gnats,
> the speck of flies,
> all in doxology together . . . great God, sovereign
> Lord. Amen.

> —*March 5, 2002, Columbia Theological Seminary*

POOR PLUTO

We learned in ancient days about the solar system.
We learned that you are the creator . . .
    you placed the sun at the center,
    and then you ordained
        Mercury and Mars and Venus and the earth,
    and at the edge of the sky, Pluto,
        the last of the planets.

We pondered the sun and its nine planets,
    and we broke out in song,
        "How great thou art!"

And now, in late-breaking news,
    we learn that Pluto no longer rates as a planet,
        downgraded to insignificance,
        hardly an orbit,
        no longer named among the big nine,
           dismissed from the big list.

The loss of Pluto on the list makes us sad and
    we grieve one of the old world dismissed.
We think of Pluto
    still spinning in space,
    still among the stars in the orbit,
        performing the tasks of creatureliness,
    but made smaller by our confident scientific labeling.

We think of poor Pluto and remember your faithfulness,
    that you love all creatures great and small,

that not a hair falls from the head but that you
    notice,
that you cherish what is mean and low and weak
    in the world,
that you remember and hope for the small ones,
    the small ones like Pluto,
        like the boys and the girls,
        like the itsy-bitsy spider,
        like the widow and the orphan and the
            immigrant,
    and all of them, like Pluto,
        demoted, relabeled, diminished, brought low.

We connect in our faithful imagination
    your mighty power
    and the small, insignificant ones;
and we are glad for your sustaining fidelity,
                for your attention to detail,
                for your capacity to preserve all
                    things
                in orderly life-giving modes.

Tend, we pray, on this day to all that is
    small and weak and vulnerable and insignificant;
we turn to you and ask for your will for shalom
    that you extend *shalom* to Pluto
        and to all whirling creatures,
    and to us.

Watch over, keep, maintain, care for, and renew . . .
and we, with Pluto, will praise you
and stay in our orbits of duty and dignity
and obedience and praise,
with joy and with thanks to you,
our creator. Amen.

—September 17, 2006

How great thou art!
How great thou art, among us . . . and we
had not noticed.
We had been busy making light of you:
    imagining our autonomy,
    craving our self-sufficiency,
    basking in our small inventions of well-being.
And then . . . in the middle of our making light,
    comes you, being heavy.
No wonder the cry goes up . . . all around us,
    cries of failure and fear,
    cries of woundedness and impotence,
    cries of vulnerability and loss.
We continue to make our way with faith-lite,
Here and there, only there and here, occasionally,
    come glimpses of your weight.
So teach us to see how the scales measure,
      and how weight is distributed.
Deliver us from our self-deceiving lightness,
      that we may reinvest in you,
      you, unforgiving,
          lordly,
          demanding . . .
you in all your weight.
How great thou art! Amen.

—February 28, 2002, Columbia Theological Seminary

ONE MORE DAY
IN OUR BIRTH PROCESS

For some small hint of sabbath rest,

For the vision that—with you—rest, not work, is our common destiny,

For your faithful keeping of promises while our world is breaking apart,

For the birth pangs of your new age
    that feel like the death pangs in our bodies,

For the cry of Jesus on the cross
    and its hint of Easter,

For all the hope you have ordained among us that we may not despair,

    For all this we thank you
    as we begin one more day and one more week
    in our pilgrimage toward ministry.

We thank you for the ministry of Jesus,
    for the energy that comes from him,
    for the example he has given us and—most of all—
    for his faithful ministry to us
        that seeks to save us from aimlessness and sin.

We are truly grateful. Amen.

—November 22, 1976

We know about your "taking away" what we value,
   taking away . . . once, twice, endlessly,
   then bereft, sad, empty.
And in the midst, you speak again,
   unexpectedly . . .
   on our behalf.
About your good intention for another day,
                  a day beyond us,
                     beyond our power,
                     beyond our knowledge,
                     nearly beyond our belief.
A good day of your fidelity toward us,
   a day of presence in all your splendor,
   a day of cleansing beyond all our failure,
   a day of shelter against all threat,
Promised by you to us . . .
   safe, beloved, protected, joyous.
Your new creation for creatures like us.
We remain for now bereft, but waiting, looking,
counting on your
   word that is our only access to newness.
   For your uttered newness among us . . .
   sometimes fleshed . . .
   we give thanks. Amen.

   — October 2, 2001, Columbia Theological Seminary

⟳⟳

Jesus loves me, this I know,
    For the Bible tells me so.
Jesus loves me in good times and in bad,
      In sickness and in health,
      In poverty and in wealth.
        Jesus loves me in my context,
        Loving us, my whole family.
    Jesus loves us, all of us Episcopalians,
    Jesus loves us, all of us Americans,
      so that "us" sometimes sounds like "U.S."
    Jesus loves and cares for our entire tribe.

But then the poetry breaks in on us and calls us out:

      O Lord my God, when I in awesome wonder
      consider all the worlds thy hands have made,
      I see the stars, I hear the rolling thunder,
      thy power throughout the universe displayed:

      Then sings my soul, my Savior God, to thee:,
      How great thou art!, How great thou art!
      Then sings my soul, my Savior God, to thee:,
      How great thou art!, How great thou art!

It turns out that Jesus loves us,
    Us and them,
    Us and non-Episcopalians,
    Us and non-Americans,
    Us who are gentle and kind and winsome,

And us who are rough and merciless, and repulsive,
Us and Jews and Muslims,
Us straight and us gay.
Jesus loves all the little children, and all the adults,
and all the radishes and rabbits and minnows and wrens.
All of us because he's got the whole world in his hands:
How great thou art; How great thou art!
And how blessed we are . . . all of us! Amen.

—*May 1, 2013, Columbia Theological Seminary, St. Timothy Church. Hymn text from Stuart K. Hine, "O Lord My God, How Great Thou Art," GtG, #625. © 1949, 1953 The Stuart Hine Trust CIO (print rights admin Hope Publishing Company, www.hopepublishing.com). All rights reserved.*

You are the source of life.
You are the giver of futures to us,
    and we do not understand why
      your power is shown us in weakness.
  We do not understand why your joy shows up
     primarily in the midst of hurt.
We are amazed that,
  time after time,
    your lordship is shown in your passion and
      suffering.
From time to time we experience you in amazement,
  but mostly we are seduced by the norms
    of success, competence, and security in our culture.
      We are nonetheless children of your history
       of hurt.
We are unsure of ourselves,
  and we yearn for security that you have not given us.
So we pray
  for the surging of your Spirit among us,
    and for the coming of newness upon your
     whole people,
     that our lives may be ordered,
     that we may rejoice after the manner of the
      crucified one.

—October 8, 1976

"Bread" (as they say in Columbus),
and all the people said, "Bread" (rising).
Bread from grain,
　　grain from soil and human toil,
　　　　　from rain and human brain,
　　　　　from sunshine and human effort,
Bread broken, shared, multiplied,
Bread without which we cannot live.
Bread blessed and given.
　　　　　　　And our energy comes back,
　　　　　　　And our good humor returns,
　　　　　　　And our best resolves are strengthened.
Bread . . . a sign, a sacrament, a surprise, a gift!
　　What do we have that we have not received?
　　(1 Cor. 4:7)
　　Well, we have received bread and we are now to
　　　　receive it again.
　　We have received bread, and meat and vegetables
　　　　and sweets.
All gifts! All inviting gratitude!
So receive bread and give thanks.
　　Ponder a while:
　　What do we have that we have not received as
　　　　pure gift?
And give thanks to the giver. Amen.

　　　　　　　　—February 5, 2015, Direct Action Resource
　　　　　　　　Training Conference, Orlando, Florida

We are, as we always are,
    preoccupied . . .
        with new ideas,
        with old fears,
        with readiness for home,
        with dread of home.

And you stand in the middle of our lives,
    vigilant,
    holy,
    demanding,
    forgiving,
    feeding.

We come now with many deep hungers;
We await your bread,
    feed us, in this very hour, till we want no more.
And nourished, cared for, loved anew,
    we will be on our way rejoicing,
        with power and courage and energy,
    our lives lived from you and lived back to you. Amen.

—January 21, 2006, Epworth By the Sea,
St. Simons Island, Georgia

(DMin Day 8)

It could be us, the people of these texts,
   because we are so like them and
     they are so like us.
It could be us,
   because we, like them,
   know about a long history
     of disobedience,
     of recalcitrance,
     of violating commands,
       not loving you alone,
       not loving neighbor,
     imagining autonomy and
     self-sufficiency.
It could be us,
   because like them we know
     about fierce judgment,
     about punishment that wells up
       among us of its own force,
  more likely we know about the judgments of
   alienation that come in
  the daily processes of life . . . even if none among
   us dare call it exile.
But then, stunningly, it could be us
   to whom you announce forgiveness.

You promise to the people of this text . . .
   it could be us . . .
   that you will forgive sin,
   that you will remember iniquity no more,
   that you will begin again,
   that you will make all things new,
   that you will bind us in gladness to your Torah,
   that we may be free of the edginess of sour
      grapes from long ago.
It could be us in disobedience and in punishment.
We pray for the freedom to marvel this day,
   that it could be us on the receiving end of your
      wondrous pardon,
   us freed and loved,
   us emancipated and redeemed,
   us brought home to well-being,
   us forgiven by you.
All this could be us . . . in the story of Jesus
                  by whom and through whom
                  you begin again. Amen.

—October 31, 2001, Columbia Theological Seminary

For your strange keeping of faith with us,

>   for the odd symmetry that surrounds us and
>   hovers over our stress,

>   for your faithful preservation of
>   summer and winter,
>   cold and heat,
>   day and night,

>   for all your abidingness while
>   our world threatens to fall apart,

>   We give you thanks.

We know that in Jesus of Nazareth all things do
indeed hang together.

We know that he is the cornerstone of your great
gift of creation. Amen.

—December 1, 1976

One time "holy,"
Two times, "holy,"
Three times, "holy,"
    All sang, "Holy, holy, holy."
Your defining adjective is beyond our understanding,
            nearly beyond our utterance,
                so awesome, so dread-filled, so beyond us.
Holy are you . . . and we become aware of our
disqualification,
                poor partners,
                unworthy worshipers,
                shabby respondents.
Holy are you . . . disqualified are we . . .
    and you call and send,
                    not to success,
                    not to pride,
                    not to security,
but to guaranteed failure: no listening,
                    no seeing,
                    no understanding,
                    no healing.
But called to the hard places that match
your holy purposes.
And we—weak, vulnerable, unsure—
we resolve to obey,
    for it is the wonder of our lives to serve
    your purpose. Amen.

    —*October 4, 2001, Columbia Theological Seminary*

⚬⚬

You have given us a time to rest,
a time to work, and
a time to play.

Day by day you call our names
and call us each time to life.

We take life from you, and we are grateful.

We thank you for the resilience of our democratic
institutions,
for the durability of our government,
for the visions of justice and peace
that dance among us.

We thank you
for the promise of new life,
for the hope that is set before us in Jesus of Nazareth:
that your kingdom will come,
that the kingdoms of this age
will become the kingdom of our God and of
his Christ.

For that sure promise we give you thanks. Amen.

—November 8, 1976

FROM PARSIMONY
TO ABUNDANCE

◦∞◦

(Genesis 12–50)

We sense an awesome mismatch
    between you and us.

You . . . all generosity and abundance and fruitfulness;
    we have heard it said of you,
        that you have more stars
        than the heavens can hold;
    we have heard it said of you,
        that you have more grains of sand
        than the beaches can bear;
    we have observed that you teem the earth
        with swarms
            of gnats and locusts and frogs,
        with swarms
            of cattle on a thousand hills,
        with swarms
            of sons and daughters,
            of calves and lambs,
                and trees.

We attest that you
    break bread and pour wine,
    and have twelve baskets full left over,
    so that our cups runneth over.

And we,
    we, grudging and fearful,
    we, counting and measuring and calculating,
    we, reckoning our worth
        and our claim
        and our possessions
        and our rights . . . against infringement.
We find our parsimony paralyzing
    and our grudging debilitating.

We present ourselves this day,
    parsimonious . . . before your abundance.

Draw us toward you and your generosity;
draw us away from our self-preoccupation;
draw us toward trust and away from fear,
      that we may be practitioners of abounding loaves,
      ready for brokenness,
      prepared to be poured out . . . and made new.

Thank you for that bodied sign of wondrous newness
    given always again. Amen.

          —October 21, 2008, Columbia Theological Seminary
                              DMin Day 2

(A Chapel Prayer)

You God of command who issues demands upon us;
You God of promise who compels us to hope;
You God of deliverance endlessly upending
    our systems of abuse;
In all your commanding, your promising,
your delivering,
    we notice your giving.
     Indeed your giving is what we notice
     first, best, and most,
       about your own life . . .
       giving without reserve or limitation.
You give us worlds of beauty and abundance,
      blessed and fruitful,
You give us sustenance for the day,
      so that we are not smitten by the sun by day
      or by the moon by night.
You give us—in the center of all your giving—
your only, well-beloved Son.
You give us your Spirit of power, energy,
and wisdom.
       Gifts all without grudging!

And we receive,
     because we have no alternative,
     because we cannot live without your gifts,
     because we have nothing but
        what you have given us.
We receive, carefully and anxiously,
     worried that there is not enough,
        of security and safety,
        of grades or grants or dollars or friends,
        of sex or beer or SUVs, of students and
           endowments,
        of futures,
        and so we crave and store up for rainy
           futures.
We receive occasionally when you stagger us
and we break beyond anxiety,
     in gratitude,
        recognizing that you in your generosity
        give us more than enough,
     and in grateful giving we become our true
        selves,
        breathed in the image of your Son.
So we ponder your generosity and are dazzled.
We measure our gratitude and our capacity to be
generous.
   We pray your haunting us beyond ourselves,
     in wonder at your way,
     in love for the world you love,
     in praise that transforms our fear,
     in wonder, love, and praise,

our lives beyond ourselves,
                toward you,
                a blessing in the world.
Hear us as we pray in the name of the
emptied, exalted One. Amen.

    —September 20, 2001, Columbia Theological Seminary

One: You are the Lord and giver of all;
      you give and give and give . . .
      all plant life,
      all animal life,
      all ocean life,
      all human life,
      teeming in fruitfulness.
      You overwhelm in abundance,

All: **We are dazzled.**

One: You give and give from your deep supply of
      bounty,
      and we cringe in fear and greed and scarcity.
      You overwhelm in abundance,

All: **We respond in life-skewing anxiety.**

One: You invite us into neighborly generosity
      with those like us and those unlike us,
      summoning us to share and trust,
      enough and more than enough.
      You overwhelm in abundance,

All: **And we debate about how much to share
      and how much to keep for ourselves.**

One: You envision neighborly justice,
      with liberty for all,
      with justice for all,
      But we keep parsing "all" into "them and us,"
      making divisions, drawing lines, rationing
      resources for life.
      You overwhelm in abundance,

 All: **And we weigh and measure and count,
      to see who deserves what.**

One: You are the Lord of all healing;
      We count on the bounty of your restorative
      power,
      And so we submit our hurts and needs and
      aches to you,
      aches of heart and body,
      So we commend to you our needful loved
      ones as we name them . . .
      You overwhelm in abundance,

 All: **And we turn to you in confidence of your
      healing capacity.**

One: You are the Lord of life
      who in your generosity has mocked the power
      of death.
      So we name our dead, and commend them to
      your bottomless mercy . . .
      You overwhelm in abundance,

 All: **We turn our small vulnerable lives over to
      your huge embrace.**

—July 26, 2015

Christ is risen! He is risen indeed!
We have glimpsed the sadness of Friday.
We have troubled the void of Saturday,
    Voids do not claim our attention very long, and
    we would not know of the void unless we knew of
      the Sunday resolution of that void.
You are the one who has broken the dark with light,
        who has dreamed peace
          amid unbearable violence;
You are the one who greets the dawn,
        who breaks the dark.
You are the one for whom
        dark and light are both alike,
         all under your sovereignty,
         all responsive to your will.
Give us grace to trust your powerful will.
Give us nerve to receive your Easter newness on
terms other than our own.
Give us joy that subverts our weary anxiety.
Give us yourself and grant that
    we shall want no more,
        no more than you. Amen.

—*April 2, 2002, Columbia Theological Seminary*

We gladly confess that you are God . . .
    full of grace and truth.
We gladly affirm that we have beheld your glory
    in the face of Jesus Christ, crucified and risen.
We gladly await your coming again,
    to turn the disobedient to the wisdom of the
        righteous, and
    to make us a people prepared.

We give you thanks that you are full of grace . . .
    that you have graced us to
        this day and this hour of hard work and clear
            thinking;
    that you have graced us amid a
    cloud of witnesses who
        wait for us,
        and watch over us;
    that you have given us a grounding in faith,
        and a deeper grounding
        in the goodness of your creation
        with its teeming generosity.

In the fullness of your grace,
    we are aware of our thin faith,
    and our shabby freedom for you.
    So override our thinness this day
            with the rush of your grace,
                that we may be free for you this day.

We give you thanks that you are full of truth,
    that you have come among us in suffering love,
    that you have settled your reliable Spirit among us,
    that you call us to be your faithful witnesses
        to your good rule of the earth.

In the depth of your truthfulness,
    we are aware of the measures of deception among us,
    as though the Prince of Lies governs our world;
    we are aware of our need for control,
        our collusions with violence,
        our fear of every threat,
    so unlike you in your reliable self.

On this day we ask you
    to surge with your grace over our fears,
    to rush with your truth amid our lies,
    that in your presence and
      in the presence of each other,
        we may become our best selves . . .
        your grace and truth
          matched by
        our wonder, love, and praise. Amen.

—September 25, 2007, Wisconsin Council of Churches,
Stevens Point, Wisconsin

MARVELING AT YOUR
SOVEREIGN GOODNESS

We marvel at you that you neither slumber nor sleep,
   that you are watchful over us in the night,
   and that you keep us in the darkness.

We marvel more at the coming of the dawn
   and at the breaking of light.

We thank you for these hours that you have
   once again put, not only at our disposal,
      but at our control.
   You have entrusted us
      with enormous power
      and magnificent freedom.

We give thanks that you also are
   God of the night which will come again,
      when we may sleep while you are awake.
   We thank you for the tasks
      you have given us today.
   We thank you for the ministry
      that you have entrusted to us.

This day we pray, through these waking hours,
  for all our colleagues in ministry,
  for all our colleagues in theological study,
    that this day
  your word may break forth with new power,
  that we and they may have discerning minds
  and open hearts,
  that the fulfillment of your yearning for justice
  may come through your people.

Amen.

—October 4, 1976

We do not understand how or why,
   but we do know that you keep your promises,
      and we know that in Jesus of Nazareth.
Your great promise of bringing life out of death,
         of calling into existence the things that do
            not exist,
         is still powerful for us.
We yearn for the coming of your promises
   in our midst,
      that you may take our chaos
         and bring order,
      that you may take our anxiety
         and bring justice,
      that you may take our scarcity
         and whelm us with abundance,
      that you may take our oppression
         and bring freedom,
      and that you may take even our dying
         and bring your great mystery of life among us.

We thank you for the coming of the rain;
we thank you for surges of healing and reconciliation;
we thank you for the many powers of nourishment
   that occur where we do not expect them.
      Because you are indeed our Lord,
         we give thanks to you.

Amen.

—September 27, 1976

We get settled as best we can,
    always a mix of quiet and turmoil,
          of ease and worry,
          of well-being and alienation.
And then . . . abruptly, inexplicably,
    You surge among us in your splendor,
    You startle us beyond our coping,
    You dazzle us beyond our control.
We had heard of your strange governance, . . .
    When you come we are blends of fear and
      gladness . . .
    We notice the newness,
          that invites and stresses us,
          that unsettles and reassures.
    You with mercy and with demand,
    You with faithfulness and with insistence,
    You in your newness, and we . . .
waiting, hoping, receiving,
    we . . . eventually glad
    and beyond our strain and fear,
          we thank,
          we praise,
          we sing,
          we exude in well-being.
Our life seized by you, broken and blessed,
          given again to us,
          on your terms . . . for our
          well-being.

More than we could ask or think or imagine,
and we begin again,
   now more fully ours,
   because we are yours. Amen.

—October 17, 2001, Columbia Theological Seminary

For hints of sabbath rest,
For the celebration of the resurrection,
For the faithful assembling of your people so that
  we do not forget,
For all the faithful people who gather week by week
  to name your name,
For the mystery of the church,
For the power of the gospel,
For the promise of ministry entrusted to us,
For Jesus Christ, hovering in strange ways among us,
  we give you great thanks. Amen.

—November 12, 1976

We give thanks.
    It is our proper posture in life,
    To acknowledge generosity.

We give thanks to God
    Who calls the worlds into being,
    Who raises the dead,
    Who calls us by name.
    Thank God—we say—it's Friday!
    We inch toward sabbath.
    We have made enough bricks,
                    enough work,
                    enough stress,
                    enough performance.
    We align ourselves with all those
        who work too hard,
        and who yearn for rest.

Thank God—we say—it's Friday!
    We inch toward Calvary and Friday death,
        Three hours of darkness,
        The curtain torn,
        The cruelty of Rome,
            And the gift of forgiveness.

Thank God—we say—it's Friday!
   We turn our thoughts back toward home and
      church,
      or we head home,
      and have home folks on our minds:
      We remember in thanksgiving
         the saints who sustain us;
      We remember in awe the ones
         who have been enslaved,
         and now know freedom;
      We remember the ones
         still treading water amid floods of chaos;
      We remember the ones
         who hope and the ones who cannot;
      We remember our ministry
         about which we are grateful,
                              or weary,
                              or provoked,
                              or all of the above.

Thank God—we say—it's Friday!
   And we inch toward a fresh time in our lives,
      more work or more rest,
      more death or more new life,
      more well-being . . . or not.
   And we say to the Lord of all our days,
      "Thanks, thanks, and thanks." Amen.

   —*October 24, 2008, Columbia Theological Seminary*
DMin Day 5

SOON!

Advent is for sharpening our senses:
    After not listening much,
      we hear angel songs again.
    After not paying much attention,
      we watch the shepherds rush to the manger again.
    After not much noticing,
      we feel the excitement of the magi,
        and the crowding of the oxen, donkeys, sheep,
        and a swan around the birth again.

Advent is for honed sensibility,
    to see, to hear, to notice, to feel.

And so to engage,
    in generosity in a culture of parsimony,
    in hospitality in a world of exclusion,
    in forgiveness in a society of revenge.

The baby ushers in a world we did not believe possible.
    That new world the baby brings
           makes for singing and dancing,
           and for gifts and risk-taking,
           and for notice of the neighbor.

All of this is soon and very soon.
We have days to make ready:

> Watching,
> Waiting,
> Hoping,
> Noticing,
> Receiving.

—Advent 2012

ON READING SAMUEL

Kingdoms rage;
empires tremble;
cities totter.
    You speak assurance;
    You designate human agents;
    You say, "This is my beloved Son";
    You say, "This is my anointed."
Right in the middle of chaos,
    you designate human agents who do your will.
And we are not sure:
    We would rather it were you,
                         directly,
                         straight on and visible.
But you stay hidden in your holy splendor,
      and we are left with human agents
      about whom we are never sure.
So we name Jesus, "Son of David";
        so human and frail, even if kicked upstairs;
        so vulnerable, even if transformed in song
          and creed.
And then, in a flash, it may dawn on us:
        You call and designate people like us, your agents.
Kingdoms rage . . . and we are called;
Empires tremble . . . and we are designated;
Cities totter . . . and we are summoned . . .
      like the first David, like the second David . . .
      us, vulnerable, frail, anxious, your people.
      And we are dazzled. Amen.

—*October 3, 2001, Columbia Theological Seminary*

You holy, you who dwell beyond us,
       you who come dwell among us,
       you unapproachable in splendor,
            hidden in light too bright,
            overwhelming in glory,
            beyond us in majesty . . .
come to abide among us in self-giving generosity,
You bending low to lodge your holiness among us.
And we, poor hosts, called to match your awesomeness,
       We match, as best we can, in purity,
                              in obedience,
                              in awe and thanks.
Our holiness, thin and shabby, as best we are able,
              acted in purity,
              acted in piety,
              acted in neighborly generosity,
              acted in hope . . .
Not adequate, fully hosting you beyond us,
              awed, silenced, yours,
              we give our "us" over to your
              "Thou." Amen.

              —*April 4, 2002, Columbia Theological Seminary*

We are a people with many words and much talk:
     creeds and
     ads and
     propaganda and
     slogans and
     sound bites.

We keep listening among these words for comfort,
     and we find ourselves made
        anxious by the cacophony.

And then . . . the din is broken;
  You speak and we enter the zone of address;
  You speak and we are called by name;
  You name and we are summoned . . .
     summoned, commanded, sent.

We hear and cringe and pause . . .
  overwhelmed by mandate.
We listen and you speak again:
  You utter words of presence,
     promises of protection,
     assurances of solidarity.

We breathe easier, still afraid,
  but on our way at risk, not alone.

Give us good ears in these days
    that we may hear the mandate
        and listen for assurance.

That even such as us may speak you well,
        you in your sovereignty,
        you in your fidelity,
        you in your sadness
            and in your newness.

Let your word be fleshed through our tongues and
            on our lips,
    that our fleshed verbiage may truly
        echo
        your word made flesh via Nazareth. Amen.

We would rather you were
    more like a nice uncle,
    more like a gentle rain,
    more like a snuggling rabbit,
    more like a windshield icon.
But you come at us . . . holy, jealous,
sometimes ferocious.
We would rather you were more like us,
    suburban, generous, forgiving, patient, caring,
    self-sufficient, not always needing our money,
                              our thanks,
                              our praise,
                              our prayers.

But then you come at us,
    Full of grace and truth and goodness.
We would like you to be our echo,
    but then we have this Jesus, you in the flesh,
    who healed and taught and fed and forgave,
    who stilled storms, and
    cast out demons, and
    rebuked hypocrites, and
    confronted governors.

We do know, down deep, that we cannot have you
on our own terms.
    Because you are before us and behind us,
      In majesty and in mercy,
      In power and in vulnerability,
      In presence and in absence.

When we think a little,
　　We can only take a deep breath and say,
　　　　"How great thou art!"
And then we take another deep breath and say,
　　"How glad we are!" Amen.

　　　　　　　　—*February 6, 2013, St. Timothy Episcopal Church,*
　　　　　　　　　　　　　　　　　Cincinnati, Ohio

(On Reading Acts 10:44–48)

One: You are the creator of all that is;
You gather all your creatures into well-being
. . . pineapples, kangaroos, deposits of oil,
eager children, slippery eels . . . all in praise.
We are grateful;

All: **And we are astonished!**

One: You gather all your human creatures into one
neighborly community, creatures of
all tongues, races, cultures, and language
groups . . . those like us and those unlike us.
We are astonished;

All: **And we are grateful!**

One: You pour out your Spirit on your church and
send us
with transformative gifts into the world.
We are astonished;

All: **And we are grateful!**

One: You pour out your Spirit on conservatives
among the baptized.
We are grateful;

All: **And we are astonished!**

One: You pour out your Spirit on liberals among
the baptized.
We are grateful;

All: **And we are astonished!**

One: You pour out your Spirit on the whole church,
all your baptized,
of every sort and condition of humanity, sent
to be
transformative, reconciling, and healing.
We are grateful that you send us;

All: **We are astonished that you send us.**

One: So we pray, give us a double portion of your
Spirit marked by energy and imagination,
Give us a triple portion of your Spirit marked
by courage and freedom and risk.
We are grateful;

All: **And we are astonished!**

One: We are dazzled that you are our mother God,
clothed in mercy and compassion;
we give thanks for our mothers made in your
image.
We are astonished;

All: We are grateful!

One: We thank you for your healing juices turned
loose in the world.
We name the healings that are happening
before our very eyes:

- Neighborliness amid violence;
- Generosity amid anxiety;
- Transformation amid despair.

We name the healings for which we yearn,
and we name those who await special
healing . . .
We are grateful for your healing force;

All: **We are astonished by your healing capacity.**

One: We remember in love our beloved dead,
Confident that they rest safely in you,
and we name them . . .
We are astonished by your faithfulness;

All: **We are grateful for your long-term embrace.**

One: Most of all, for the good news of the gospel,
we give you great thanks.
Hear our gratitude for your goodness;

All: **Hear our astonishment at your unfailing mercy!**

—May 10, 2015

SCRIPTURE INDEX

This Scripture index for the three volumes in the Collected Prayers of Walter Brueggemann series includes both quotations from and references to the listed texts in the forewords and prayers.

OLD TESTAMENT

Genesis

8:22	116 (2)
9:8–17	116 (1)
12–50	80 (3)
12:1–3	xvii (2)
12:10	111 (2)
33	23 (2)
37	56 (1)

Exodus

1–15	26, 28 (2)
2:23	xxi (1); xvi (3)
3–4	25 (2)
7–12	62 (3)
10	78 (2)
15	30 (2)
15:17	xviii (2)
15:20–21	xviii (2)
15:21	xvi, xvii (3)
16:2–5	111 (2)
19–24	32 (2)

20:1–6	110 (1)
20:4–6	48 (1)
20:8–11	125 (2)
20:17	48 (1)
32:11–13	xvii (1); xviii (2)
32:14-17	xvii (1)
33:12–23	xviii (2)
34	xxviii (1)
34:6–7	xxvi (1)
34:9–10	xviii (1)

Leviticus   127 (2)

Numbers

14:13–19	xxviii (1); xviii (2)
14:18	xxvi (1)
14:20	xxviii (1)

Deuteronomy 44 (1); 35 (2)

5:12–15	129 (2)
6:4	38 (1)
16:20	xxxii (1)

Joshua		73	54 (1)
5:12	111 (2)	74	78 (1); 104 (2)
21:43–45	xviii (2)	77	147 (2)
		88:9	xxv (1)
1 Samuel	37 (2);	88:13	xxv (1)
	100 (3)	96	93 (3)
3	39, 131 (2)	96:10–13	xxxiv (1)
3:19–21	74 (1)	104:10–11	14 (1)
5	40 (2); 67 (3)	107	93 (3)
8	42 (2)	109:9–13	xxiv (1)
12	88 (1); 92 (2)	117	xxiii (1)
		130	91 (1)
2 Chronicles		145	45 (2)
36:23	xix (2)	146	50 (3)
		150:3–6	xxiii (1)
Ezra			
9	xx (2)	**Isaiah**	
		1	76, 77 (1)
Nehemiah		1–2	11 (1)
9	xx (2)	1:21–26	137 (2)
		3	93 (2)
Psalms	72 (1); 43, 79,	4:2–6	xii, 69 (3)
	81 (2)	5:20	61 (2)
15	135 (2)	6	83 (2); 78 (3)
22:1	xxv (1)	9:2–7	95 (2)
24	135 (2)	11:1–9	136 (2)
30	xvi, 42 (3)	14:24–27	47 (2)
30:5	xvi, xvii (3)	25	61 (1)
30:8-10	xvi (3)	28	61 (1)
30:11	xvi (3)	39	80 (1)
30:12	xvi (3)	40:9–11	81 (1)
35	149 (2)	46–47	90 (1)
44:23	xxv (1)	49:14–15	xx (1)
44:26	xxv (1)	49:15	28 (1)
46	78 (1)	55:1–2	112 (2)
54	12 (1)	55:12	xix (2)
68:5	28 (1)	56:3–8	107 (1)

64:1–9	96 (2)	**Joel**	
65:24	xxi (1)	3:10	11 (1)
Jeremiah	52 (1);	**Amos**	
	49 (2)	8:4–8	38 (1)
2–3	141 (2)		
3	51 (2)	**NEW TESTAMENT**	
3:1–4:4	53 (2)		
8:18–9:3	55 (2)	**Matthew**	
9	64 (1)	11:28	135 (2)
9:10–22	143 (2)	13:52	xiii (2)
9:23–24	xxi (3)	23:23	xxxiii (1)
11:18–12:6	xix (2)	27:46	xxv (1)
14	14 (1)		
14:19	14 (1)		
15	98 (2)	**Mark**	
15:10–21	xix (2)	1:17	xxi (2)
15:18	xviii (1)	2:14	xxi (2)
17:5–11	57 (2)	6:30–44	110 (2)
17:14	xviii (1)	8:1–10	110 (2)
17:14–18	xix (2)	8:17	110 (2)
18:18–23	xix (2)	8:31	xxii (2)
20:7–13	27–29 (3)	8:34	xxi (2)
20:7–18	xix (2)	9:30–32	xxii (2)
20:13	xviii (1)	10:21	xxi (2)
23	59, 61 (2)	15:34	xxv (1)
25	99 (1)		
29	103 (1)	**Luke**	
30–31	114 (1)	1:53	112 (2)
31:20	63 (2)	9:1	xxii (2)
31:31–34	xii, 75 (3)	10:9	xxii (2)
32	65 (2)	10:17	xxii (2)
36	112 (1)	24:36–43	60 (3)
52:31–34	67 (2)		
		John	
Hosea		16:20–22	xvii (3)
2:19–20	xvi (1)		

Acts
3:1–16   62 (1)
10:44–48   106 (3)
24:14   xxi (2)

Romans
8:28   24 (3)

1 Corinthians
4:7 xxii (1); 115 (2); 73 (3)

2 Corinthians
8:1–15   45 (2)

Galatians
5:22–23   xxi (3)

Ephesians
6:12   xxxii (1)

Philippians
2:1–11   26 (1)

3:1   xii, xx (3)
4:4   xii, xx (3)
4:6   xxii (1);
                xx (3)
4:7   xx (3)
4:10   xx (3)
4:18   xx (3)

1 Thessalonians
5:17–18   xxii (1)

Hebrews
11   137 (2)
11:13–16   xx-xxi (2)
11:39–40   xxi (2)

1 John
3   69 (2)

Revelation
22:20   xxxiii (1)

9 780664 268282